How To Improve SEO (search engine optimization)
By
Matthew Silva

Introduction

There are many different ways that you can improve you websites Search Engine Optimization or SEO. SEO can help you to get your website at the very top of google, yahoo and other well known search engines. Whenever you begin creating your new website than you need to keep in mind all of these upcoming tips inorder to make your website strong for SEO from beginning to end. The tips that are provided here will not guarantee you get to the top of google or yahoo, but will greatly improve your current SEO situation. SEO can greatly increase the hits on your site, which in turn will increase your business means. Becoming fluent with these tips on improving your SEO will greatly benefit you on your future projects. Trust me when I say that making sure your SEO is as good as it can be, is more rewarding than can be imagined, espcaially today in the internet era, it is manditory to be SEO efficent.

It is a very good idea for a person developing there website to consider the keywords being used in every facet. A website that is very rich with keywords will help to improve SEO. Another thing that is a must is doing a good amount of reasearch about the keywords you are choosing to use. There are many differnt ways that you can research which keywords are used most often. Finding the keywords that are used most often will help you to decide which keywords to use throughout your site. This is a great thing for anyone because this will make sure your keywords are useful instead of useless. There are SEO tools that are available for you to use such as Gooogle Adwords Keyword Tool and Keyword Discovery. Using these tools will help you to see which keyowords are most popular in search engines. Using the most effective keywords will only greatly increase your websites SEO.

Another key thing that will help you with your SEO is to understand that you must actaully have a site with good content. Whatever your site contains must be wanted by people and also creative. Your content must be good and also up to date, this will be a very vital thing to your SEO. Having great content will help you impress the viewers of your website. Making sure that your viewers are happy should always be the key idea to your website and having this idea should also help with your SEO. Making a blog within your site, is a very good idea for some of the content that should be within your sites. Blogs are loved by many of the larger search engines and should be apart of your website in some way or fashion if you want to have SEO improvment. Also make sure that the blog that you are using is not through a 3rd party website or they will be receiving the SEO boost from it.

The next thing that you need to know is that you need to be aware of Google Analytics. This is a free software analytics package. Google Analytics will give you many differant tools. You need to make sure the the html for your Google Analytics to your website is attached to every page of the site. This will track how many people are viewing the site. Also by using Google Analytics you can see which key words and search engines are producing hits for your website. This data is also going to be used for further bettering your site in the future. Another key thing that you will want to do is to make sure that you try to register and host your domain with a very repuatable webhost. If you are with a very tacky webhost that is putting your website on the same server as pornographic websites or other websites that google does not like than your website is bound to be guilty by association.

Having many links to your website is very important for your search engine optimization. Links are very important for search engine optimization they also have always been a very important value to getting a higher ranking on search engines. If you have a link on The LA Times to your website, it is worth more than many blogs. When you also have links within your sites pages between different parts they can help link authority from one page to another, this will give search engines a good sign the pages are grouped together. You can also do networking by trying to volunteer to offer your content for others websites. Another thing that you should be warned of is that you should never buy a link, or use spamming techniques, or use third-party forms, or use directory listings, etc. search engines are very good at seeing these types of strategies and ignoring them. Social media can also be very important for search engine optimization. The importance of the popular social media companies such as Facebook, twitter, Instagram, Pinterest, LinkedIn and Google+ should not be ignored.

It is very important for you become familiar with these social media companies, and also to make an account with them listing your business and its mission. Promoting yourself is very good for your business, and also for your websites search engine optimization. Search engines such as Yahoo and Bing are using social signals as a ranking signal, which means that if you are popular on Facebook and other popular social media websites than you will improve your websites search engine optimization.Make sure that the code that you are writing for your website is not excessive. Excessive code will slow down your website loading time, and will also increase the possibility of errors in the coding. All of your files such as scripts and CCS files should be added as external files which will reduce the time it takes for search engine spiders to find the content as well as reducing the code to content ratio.This is mainly not to have a direct impact on your website search engine optimization but make it an easier time for search engine's spiders.

Another very important thing to make your website the best it can be for search engine optimization is to make sure that each page is a very unique. You do not want to duplicate content on different pages in the same website. Having very relevant content that you cannot find in other places on the Internet is very key when Google ranks a website. Other than having the same information with the pages on the same website you do not want to have the same information that other people have on their websites, you want your content to be as original as possible. Duplicate content is very possible and will happen, but do your best in order to make your content original and different from the rest. The algorithm that Google uses is made to find new and relevant content. If This algorithm notices that your content is the same as another websites it may run the risk of your website being ignored. When you are using content this should remove your worries about your site being ignored by Google's spiders. You also do not want to cut and paste bits of information from other webpages on to your website because this will also count against you and your search engine rankings.

Having this problem duplicating information that someone finds off the Internet is very hard to overcome, the Internet is a plethora of information that you can learn new things from and share with others. There's information on the Internet that you want to share on your website or duplicate in a way, the best thing that I have found to do is to memorize the information and rewrite it in your own unique wording.

You also want to use meta-tags throughout your website. Having these meta tags will be the first chance for you to attract new visitors, it will also give descriptions of what your website is about. These description tags are also used by Google to differentiate between webpages, which also brings back the importance of using unique content for your description tags so that you do not run into duplication issues. Another thing to make sure that you realize is to limit the length of your description tags to around 160 characters. Having very unique and descriptive tags will help you attract visitors, and improve your search engine optimization rankings.

By making many listings and even trying to make listings in your local governments listing areas, you will greatly improve your chances of getting a much better rank for search engine optimization. Another thing that can highly boost the effectiveness of your website is allowing your listings that you just added to local search engine and directories, to add reviews by the viewers. You would also benefit from adding a review section on your website. Also knowing that your content is going to help boost your search engine optimization, sometimes it is very beneficial for companies to offer free product or services of some kind. When people are searching for your product and realize that it may be for free then you will get a mass amount of viewers which will highly increase the rank of your search engine optimization.

Making sure that you are delivering the best website and product to your customer is going to make your customers happy and also search engines. Today people are using Mobile phones in mass quantities, which are available to search the web on these devices. Having a mobile website which is connected to your desktop website, can also improve the experience that your customers have, which will also greatly raise your rank in search engine optimization. Another thing that will be very important when you try to improve your search engine ranking is to realize that you have available to you the option to create an XML site map. When creating an XML site map this will be the list of URLs on your website. When you submit these to Google's Webmaster tools you ensure that you will be providing all of your webpages there are on your website, which is giving it a chance to discover and label your content.

Another thing that you can do in order to create A better website which in turn gives you a better ranking in search engines, Is to create a favicon. By creating a favicon you will be branding your website, it'll also be making your website look more elegant due to the favicon in the corner of the window as opposed to a blank sheet of paper. Having a favicon is very important because this makes your website look professional and up to standards.

Another thing that can greatly benefit your website is to network off-line. Today if you go out and meet people and go to local networking events than you may have a better chance to advertise your website. When getting to know new people opportunities rise, because when meeting people you have opportunities such as them blogging on your website which will greatly and improve SEO.

Another thing that you should think about when trying to improve your websites SEO is the navigation within your site. It should be your goal to make your viewers trip through your website as smooth and as uncomplicated, that their journey should be. It seems that usually the shorter steps it takes in order to find your contact details and complete a sale, is going to give your website a very high success rate. It is also known that when search engines use spiders they tend to crawl to your website just as a viewer would navigating through your website using navigation links, so if the people who view your website are having a good time browsing through, it is a good chance that the search engines crawlers are also going to.

Another thing that you can do in order to boost your search engine optimization, is to get listed on all of the local search engines and directories. It is always a good idea to start with very huge companies such as the Yahoo directory and Google plus.

Again I would like to touch base on the keywords for your website. You want to focus on keywords that are very high in volume but have fairly low competition. You also want to use keywords with long tails. Usually when people search for something it is about 2-4 keywords long. It will also benefit the ranking of your search engine optimization if you analyze other websites that are similar to your own. By analyzing these websites that are similar to your own website you may discover new keywords that you may want to target.

when search engines use their crawling software to read websites information, It must be technically perfect. If your website information is not technically perfect then it will be much more difficult for this crawling software to read your information. If the crawler cannot understand your content this will have a very negative effect on your search engine optimization, giving you a lower ranking or a zero ranking.

Now that you have made sure that your content is relevant and very good it is also important to make sure that your content is not outdated. It is very bad if you had outdated content. This will greatly have a negative effect on your search engine optimization. Make sure that you update your content regularly. Updating everything within your site is very important to slowly move up the ranks in search engines. Another thing that is very important is to have creative topics on your blog. It is very important to have topics for people to become interested in so that they can use your blog. When people are chatting on your blog then your website will definitely increase in its search engine rankings. I also believe that the quality of your blog is very important. People want to leave posts so that others can respond to it. If this is not done correctly then it will discourage people from using a blog this will result in a lowering of your search engine optimization ranking.

Another thing that is vital for you to do to increase your search engine ranking is to understand that you should have styles and labels for your paragraphs, Objects and headings. When you have your styles labeled with things such as h1,h2,p1, and p2 this will make it much easier for crawlers to navigate throughout your website. Once again better helping your chances to increase in the search engines ranking.

It's also very important to understand that you do not want to cheat your way to the top of search engines catalogs, although you really want to have credible content with your keywords. Do not duplicate keywords throughout your website just so you have a huge number of them, crawlers can recognize this and may put your website on the low end of the totem pole when it comes to search engine optimization this a very bad thing.

When trying to make your website try to build it with the flash being a minimum. I do realize that people do highly enjoy reading flash, but search engines do not. Search engines try to skip right over flash. It is also very bad for phone traffic.

It is very bad to design your website so that search engines see one thing and your viewers see different things than the search engine does. In the technical world we would call this cloaking. This would be done when you redirect or you do this with programming, this is forbidden by Google. When you're tricking people with redirection it is not fun for anyone. When someone is looking to ride horses and they are redirected to the site about crocheting then this is a way of trickery. When you cloak your website it is very bad, and will most likely get you banned from Google. Being banned from Google is very bad because you will not be found by many viewers at all.

Another bad idea is to have a robot write your website. Today it is possible to get a machine to write content for you. There are many programs available out there that usually duplicate the same content over and over but make very minor minute changes to the code. When Google sees this it is very possible for them to ban your website and for you to get a very very low ranking in search engines. You can also use websites and other companies to use their programming in order to use templates for websites. Using these templates is a also very bad idea in order to become a higher ranked website in search engines.

This is because once again you are duplicating a website over and over with very minute changes to the website. Google can recognize this and will punish you for it, giving you a very little ranking in their search engine. Another very bad idea is to hide your text and keywords for making the background color the same as the font color. When you make the background color the same as the font color by hiding the text this is called font matching. When you decide to become a font matcher you will be looked down upon by Google and other search engines which are increasingly sophisticated at catching these types of maneuvers. They will most likely remove any websites doing this. It Is also a very bad idea to make very tiny text throughout the website that isn't visible by viewers, containing many keywords, this will result in the same thing as font matching.

It is also another good thing for you to include content in your site that answers questions that are relevant to the viewer. First of all it is always good to answer questions such as what is your site all about and what do you offer, how expensive are your services or goods, are you reliable, what is your background and do you have any experience, what are your goals, how are you to be reached, Is it easily to reach you.

Another very good thing that you can do to help boost search engine optimization is to interlink sites that you already have. When you have multiple sites it is very wise to link these sites together through links that you create. When you create multiple sites that link together this is a great way away to control the linking solely by yourself. This will advertise your websites online through each other making your search engine rankings rise.

Another thing that is very important is that you need to understand is to link your social networking sites that are associated with your website to the website. This is a very big mistake I have seen many people do, not linking their website to the Facebook or other social media website that is associated with it. Being on Twitter or on Facebook can help your search engine ranking but I personally think that when you link your website to the social networking website that your website is associated to, Then this will do you greater good than actually just being on the site.

Also when designing your website you want to be plentiful with alt tags. When you are describing either your visual media or video media you are going to be sure you're using alt tags. This is a very big deal because many search engines today locate your page through these alt tags. This means that you will be recognized easier if you include these alt tags, furthermore rising your ranking with search engines.

Another key very important thing is to make sure that you are aware of Google plus. Google plus is used as a type of social media website. Google plus can also help you to highly boost your search engine ranking on Google's very large search engine. Whether you happen to be a internet marketer or a webmaster Google plus will be a very large part of your SEO plans.

Google plus is here to connect social communication people to build your websites ability to rank higher on search. I could keep going on and on about the importance of goole plus, but for now I am going to give you just some quick tips about how to optimize your google plus. First of all when making a Google plus profile you want to make sure that the profile is good. Make sure that you're completing all the required fields that it asks you to complete when filling out your Google plus profile for the first time. It is also a very good idea to link your Google plus page to your own websites and other social sites.

The content that you post on Google plus should be of high-quality and relevant to your business or website. You also want content you're posting to engage your audience which will also cause your viewers to have less of a bounce rate. With these few tips I Advise you further research Google plus on your own when having available time. Making sure that your google plus profile is as optimized as possible is very important to your search engine ranking. Once again it is very important for you to become familiar with Google plus in wanting to achieve a higher search engine ranking on one of the largest search engines in the world which is Google. Not having an understanding of google and the way it works is going to be a very critical downfall to your website and your business.

Another thing you want to do to boost your website is to market and advertise it. There are many ways you can market your website. First off you can always market your website in the real-world. When you get out into the real world and talk to people and tell them about your website by word-of-mouth than this can be a way to gain more views. You can also market your website on your vehicle, on your Business card, by wearing T-shirts with your website on it, by wearing hats with your website on it. Tell all of your friends and family about your new website and tell them to visit it. It is very important to your website to also be social in real life. Today many people are social online, forgetting that the real world is out there also. To maximize your potential when advertising your website and marketing it you will-want to make sure that your advertising yourself on social media websites and also being social in real life. By doing these two things you'll gain friends and also their views. In the end this will greatly increase your search engine rankings online.

Throughout this book I've shown you many different ways that you can improve your search engine ranking. Although I do want to make sure that you are not overwhelmed with all of these steps. I would advise you that you take one thing at a time and optimize it to the best of your ability before you move onto the next step. You don't half ass many things, Whole ass one thing. If you do this and follow this advice then I would imagine your search engine ranking Will soon be much higher than it was before. I have known many people who follow these steps precisely and vigorously to increase their views of page by 2000 percent. Once again I want to emphasize how important it is to make sure that your content is relevant to the subject of your website, and that it is also great content. You need your content to be original and great, this is my last advice before ending the book, content is king.

www.ingramcontent.com/pod-product-compliance
Lightning Source LLC
Chambersburg PA
CBHW070929050326
40689CB00015B/3682